BALLOTS FROM THE DEAD

Poems by J.J. Tindall
Selected from the *Beachwood Reporter*

Published by Beachwood Media Company, Inc., Chicago, Illinois.

Copyright ©2010 by J.J. Tindall

All rights reserved. No part of this book may reproduced in any form or by any electronic or mechanical means, including information storage and retrieval systems, without permission from the publisher, except by a reviewer, who may quote brief passages of the text.

Design and cover photograph by Sheila Sachs

ISBN 978-0-557-52532-4

For Steve, Bob, Jane
and Mom

And for
CDR Dan F. Shanower, USN
February 2, 1960 – September 11, 2001

Praise for J.J. Tindall's poetry:

"Tindall's audiopoetry embraces both the pop and aesthetic/artistic lines of contemporary spoken word. Therein he has found success in creating work that is accessible to laypeople, while rendering ample ideas and subtle innovations for more critical listeners."
—Kurt Heintz, e-poets.net

"Jim Carroll and Patti Smith—poets who channeled the rawness and sprit of rock 'n' roll into their works—are the easiest reference points for performer J.J. Tindall . . . A portrait of Chicago that locates a bit of beauty amidst the industrial ugliness."   —*Illinois Entertainer*

"Tindall's phrases are diligently expanded into great overarching structures of metaphor, draped with banners of imagery and bristling with intricate and exquisite turns of phrase."   —ChicagoPoetry.com

Foreword by Steve Rhodes

YOU HAVE BEFORE YOU the greatest collection of American poetry published in the new millennium. By a Chicago author. For a Chicago website. If you like that sort of thing.

But then, maybe, truly, it is the best-in-class. After all, who else can claim *Ode to a Hoover Bagless Cyclonic Action Quik-Broom with On-Board Tools* ("Quiet machine, soft machine, I machine") in the same breath as *Five Boys On a Golf Course* ("We who remained drove a van to Arlington, VA, for the military funeral, smoking joints and telling stories. The Navy bore pall for us all.")?

J.J. Tindall's "Chicagoetry" collection is at once hyperlocal and universal, teenaged and adult, desperate and thoughtful, familiar and only sometimes a little bit strange.

"I crave release from the heft of dreams," J.J. writes in "Carnivale."

J.J.'s dreams are heavy, but must they be so? No reader with any depth of soul could think so. His poetry is about the constant interference by outside forces of those things which we–he–really cherish. Or ought to. A life of dreams shouldn't be so hard when the dreams are so real.

CONTENTS:

Wonderland 1
My New Job 2
Pigeon 4
Intimations 5
Black Spring 6
Rain 7
Dream Diary 8
A Murder of Tulips 10
The Cloud Ulysses 11
Ode to a Hoover Bagless Cyclonic Action Quik-Broom
    with On-Board Tools 12
Carnivale 14
White Dream 16
Shangri-La Shattered 18
Illumination 19
Oasis 20
Gleam 22
Bad 23
Funeral for a Bastard Year 24
Life 25
Elegy for Studs 26
I Want to Lick Tequila Off Your Thighs 28
Get the Lions 29
Life with Bon Scott 30
Silent Supernova Symphony 32
Five Boys on a Golf Course 33
All Saints Triptych (Homage to Skrebneski) 36
Wish You Were Beer 43
Great Expectations 44
The Great Black Diamond 46
Led Zeppelin at the Stadium, Easter Sunday, 1977 48
Prospectus: My Jimmy John's on Baghdad's Magnificent Mile 50
I Once Prayed to God 52

49 Western Owl Fever Dream	53
The Moon Wanes Over the Lagoon	54
I Was Watching Jim Miklaszewski	55
The Rod Beck Bummer	56
Rainbow Over the Adler from an Omnibus	57
The Hawk	58
Allen Ginsberg Festival of Life	59
My Good War	60
Depression	62
Men Made Out of Birds	63
The Conquest of Shit Creek	64
The Great White Dope	65
The Heart is a Lonely Fucker	66
Feed My Steel Bird	67
Baker Street Blues	68
Living in a Little Catholic Cemetery	70
Pindaric Ode to the Fantastic Four	71
How Could I Not Seethe?	72
I Dreamed I Saw St. Valentine	74
Dudes	75
After Midnight in the Latin Quarter	76
Gimme Back My Bullets	77
The Governor's Whore	78
Mighty Santo at the Bat (The Cubs Will Shine in '69)	79
Elegy for White Power	80
A Modest Proposal	83
My Silver Soul the Sea	84
Division Street: Two Americas	85
Barshomba and the Green Bunny	86
Bronze Gilead	88
Black Dog in Little Hell	90
Regulated Militia Well	91
Beachwood Hamlet	92

WONDERLAND

So I got fired and may lose my home.
I wonder why it has to be so hard.
The very December wind now hounds me,
chilling visions of homelessness abound.
I wonder "why now?" I wonder "so how
do I party with the holiday crowd?"
Life takes no holiday. Life is this hard.
My sense of self has imploded in shards.
But I must smile my way through the season
and I must guile my way through cold reason.
The garish December sun gives no warmth
though after Solstice light again comes forth . . .

MY NEW JOB

My new job
is finding
my new job.

My new office
is straddling
my small crib.

"Get up early, be flexible, network in person, stay positive."
Jesus: stay positive.

When I'm kicking ass,
you don't have to tell me twice
"This, too, shall pass."

When my ass is kicked
you can't tell me
it won't last.

"Stay positive." Jesus H. Christ.
  * * * * *

Hobbled, humbled, humiliated.
"I'm a highly-motivated self-starter and a great team player who
thrives on a challenge."

Disposed, disposable, dispossessed.
"I believe my experience, creativity and professionalism makes me a
strong candidate for the position."

Hungry, harried, hopeworn.
"My skill set, maturity and ability to stay focused under pressure . . . "

Busted, boned, bereaved.
"Please feel free to contact me at your convenience to further adioh
fapsodbnl; oajdbnf;lakn lskeninf'lien'

l;inf'ldinf al;isdl f asl;dknf;aosine;r nfnoas

FUCK! I need some
air.
  * * * * *
I found a new path
to the gazebo,

east of the boulevard,
south of the creek.

I ditched my dreams —
yeah, I DITCHED MY DREAMS —

of brook trout for breakfast
and new shoes by the front door.

I flew the coop, fled
the cot

in the
cubicle.

I rode my bummer
to the park

to let it
go.

I flounced upon the frozen gazebo,
leaned back against a stone arch
and let it

go.

It took
some time . . . my mind like a gull strafed
the white solid sea,
the undulating fields, the denuded
groves.

It took
some time . . . but then the blind gull
skywrote a
hard-rhyming
song:

"Success: finite.
Joy: finite.
Failure: finite.
Sorrow: finite.

Coda?
Interlude.
Hard stop?!
INTERLUDE.
Winter:
Winterlude.

It'll take
some time,

but this, too,
shall pass."

PIGEON

I scanned a bronze and teal pigeon at loiter on the black snow.
I blanched at reports from a pistol in the alley.
I remain enhanced, wait, enchanted

By the night skyline
Pixelated

On the
Bleak

Black
Lake.

INTIMATIONS

Rescue cannot be summoned,
Captivity must be endured.
The bastard wind our gaoler
Retains jurisdiction, random
Beatings loom, black ice
Lurks.

But the Wind Warden's power is waning
And the block walls
Are slowly, slowly melting. The light is waxing
And the pastels of renewal (lavender,
Rose, budding emerald) have returned
At least to my shivering, grey-scale dreams.
The body knows if the heart still longs.
Rotten drifts, salt-encrusted fenders,
Street trash revealed

Seed the grey clouds with warm rain.
The tyranny of assaulting air
Will lash out as it dies away, but
The broad lake, which rebuffs
The extremes of Canadian gales,
Will prevail.

BLACK SPRING

I forgot I love you.
There was a star
Above your manger
And I followed it to the Empty Bottle.
Mammals re-emerged from the air-raid shelters
Toward the buzz drone ragas

Of Red Red Meat. Bleary-eyed,
Bewildered by loss and doom,
Re-animated by the stark miracle

Of Warmth.
Fangs stained by
Tar and rain,

Blood warmth twirling under black
Stars. It is spring but it is black.
It is black but it is spring it is spring.

Men bloated and grey-haired,
Women still beautiful beautiful.
I was doing "The Air Stream Driver"

To "Air Stream Driver!" Develop
A dance! Word leaked out
That warmth returned. Word.

Tom toms: gargantuan.
Steel strings: Olympian.
Blistering ragas bled us

Of our tension dreams and mute,
Mortal terror in the stale, stooped
Night. I forgot I love you,

Wicked winter. I forgot I love!
Leaking blue books
And wild mares in heat,

Buzz drones bleat us along
Toward our brittle manger.
Fangs and mange, swirling drones,

Mammals bearing crosses
Of shimmering stars back
To the bars.

RAIN

I can show you
that when it rains and shines
it's just a state of

mind. But life is
mind and
mind

is real.
When the sky closes,
a million I's become

one wet We,
temporarily trapped
in a Brigadoon Atlantis.

Bass notes in our blood
resonate to the visiting
kin,

buds of blues emerge,
brain-clouds drape the skyline
in God,

humbling these
monuments to brittle
ego.

Sun is bright
and rain is blue,
sun is right
and rain is true.

Sun is Saturday,
faith, Lincoln, cheer.
Rain is Sunday,
doubt, Grant, fear.
And these are just

states of mind
but absolutely real

as faith

and fear.

DREAM DIARY

I was an extra
in the new Batman movie
along with Amy Sedaris,
and we were filming a scene
in the rain near Wayne Manor
(a Mock Tudor mansion in West
Humboldt Park, south of Fullerton)
featuring Benicio del Toro.

The Joker made an appearance
and the papparazzi turned out to be
his crew of henchmen
turning their cameras into guns.

Then there was a scene in which
the Joker, an older Hispanic man,
and his main henchmen —
including Benny made up as Mr. Hyde —
met around a table. Then, after the shoot,
we went to Benny's large, old Victorian
house near the scene location,
where he was living with
a couple of Hispanic dudes.

"You could live your whole life
on the West Side,"

Benny said. One dude was applying cocaine
from a small, wax paper packet to wounds
on the bald head of the other dude
who'd been beaten by police.
Something had gone wrong with their
inside coverage.

Then Benny took me up to the roof
and we got into his '60s convertible.
He drove us around the roof,
getting closer and closer
to the edge.

Finally, he drove us off the third story
onto the yard below.
I braced for my stomach to drop
but it didn't happen,
and we landed safely,
back-end first.

Then Amy was on her bike
getting ready to leave
and we made out.
I wanted to go back
to Wayne Manor so
I would remember

where it was . . .

A MURDER OF TULIPS

I lug my spavined heart
to work
along the Magnificent Mile.
A murder of tulips
belies my grief.
They are nothing!

Still, serene, stoic, superlative.

A murder of tulips
defies my grief, I cannot
unshine them, I cannot

unsee them.
Green winged angels with yellow halos

perform a harrowing visual requiem.
A brace of supple choirs

enact a vivid, visceral psalm.
The do no thing for me!
But they are themselves.

CHICAGO IS EGO!
And yet they sing.
MY RESUME IS OBSOLETE!
And yet they sing.
MY FAITH IS INCOMPLETE!
And yet they sing.

And yet they sing:
"If the idea
of God
is God
let it be
God.

If the idea
of Hope
is Hope
let it be
Hope."

They do nothing for me!
They are better than me.

And they sing.

THE CLOUD ULYSSES

His name
was Hiram.
He won
a war.

He is buried
in Grant's Tomb.
He lives
in Grant Park.

I sometimes see
his cloud galloping
gamely along
the lake.

ODE TO A HOOVER BAGLESS CYCLONIC ACTION QUIK-BROOM WITH ON-BOARD TOOLS

I and I: machine.
Quiet machine, soft machine,
I machine.

Quiet machine:
a mongrel corpus
of wills.

Every street light up Pulaski
for forty blocks
is lit!

The grid breathes.
But you have to
breathe!

You have to breathe.
Cyclones in
bottles,

one by one,
a corridor of white
fire

vanishing
gamely into the blue-black
horizon.

Steel brick and
mortar channel the changeling
gust,

the soft, spring
southerly Gulf gust: it comes
from the Gulf!

Tear duct
of Quetzlcoatl! Blue ruby
of Ra!

Yeah: for the most part,
a lot quieter now,
if you

factor in
the Dynamo
Hum.

Ah! The HUM.
It burnishes the gust.
Dynamos wreaking

havoc only sometimes
it's benevolent havoc, it
works out.

The paid stay
paid, the rich stay
rich

so the machine
is that much more efficient
and way, way

quieter.
I and I gorge
on materiel!

I and I swoon
in the burnished breeze!
That's machine,

too, don't
forget (what if you could finally NOT
FORGET?!).

Surely machine,
too, that swoon were
I and I

to testify.

CARNIVALE

I hate my hurt
I hate my lies
I crave light wait
I crave lightness

I crave release
from the heft
of dreams, from the cruel
realities of
desire

the death of me
sets me free
the death of you
that's news

the breath of you
that's truth
I am bereaved
by the theft
of you

cleaved
by the less
of you

the press of yearning
I hate this weight
but it is life, but is time
I crave the bright
I crave the best
of you

I ache
to fly

alone above the skyscrapers
temples and tombs
light released unleashed
from grief
it's true

I have my hurt
I have my lies

honed by hurt
hammered by lies
light like a dragonfly's
wing

stung by light
stunned by incessant unfathomable
longing
I dream of no dreams
free light no

news no
wings

WHITE DREAM

Dreams come
in clouds, floating through
the blue

brain. There goes fame,
there fortune, there
beautiful

lovers. Light,
lithe, invigorating
clouds

(quiet, not loud).
Black clouds fly,
white clouds

float, each
an invention
of self.

Many clouds
borrowed money from their dad
and came

to Chicago.
To invent
themselves.

There goes Augie Swift,
there Louis Sullivan, there
(MY FAVORITE) Montgomery

Ward. So
here I and I
came.

To the City of
White Dreams, City
of Inventors.

Came
to invent
myself.

Here is Billy
Corgan, here
Michael Jordan, here

Oprah.

I want
to be cool,
too!

Aw, shucks.
My cloud
keeps crashing

into the lake,
baptized by
failure.

My dad
is dead now so I can't borrow any more
dough.

Yet I and I
persist, re-inventing
ramp, breeze

and brass
balls. CITY OF
BRASS

BALLS.
Narcissus of
Cloudgate, sure, sure.

I and I breathe
to shine
on you,

seethe
to shine
on you,

vying,
though
vexed,

to
glide.

SHANGRI-LA SHATTERED

Look: tatters. Tattered
concrete coat upon
steel-rod sticks.

Leave it shattered,
the shuttered Shangri-La Hotel,
ersatz Shamabala

starting at six hundred
grand. It matters.
Leave it: husk

of a hoary hard-on
replete with billboards
and price-points.

Botch without bang,
dry whistle whimper
late to the orgy,

stately pleasure dome
diseased. Leave it
rot by the river

where everyone can see.
As in a crucifixion,
leave rot a cautionary

corpse, a shining for fools.
Hallow what is wrought
when luxury for a few

marauds mercy for the many.
Leave it rot so we
NEVER FORGET that wrought.

ILLUMINATION

I strove to summon the gods
with cliches of madness. Pose after pose, put on after put on,

point of view after
point of view.
Then the Old Post Office became a sphinx
in a late dawn

lavender. Merely a vision,
not madness.
A reflex of imagination
from a cache of outrage.

Anger, not madness.
To feel illuminated by the force of God's will.
To reel, exhumed.

OASIS

for Margaret Patch

O: that's my SELF
floating before me
content and contrite,
liberated by quietude
and the slant
of autumn light.

Only in absentia
do I realize the drum
of the incessant, urban
Dynamo Hum.
Suddenly: a sea
change . . .

cicadas for sirens,
whippoorwills for
car alarms,
playing cards in bike spokes
for Mack trucks on
potholes.

I don't miss the tamale
stands, tire shops
and bars
but it's only Oak Park
so I still can't see
the stars above

the hemlock, juniper,
evergreen, oak,
aspen, juniper,
catalpa and birch.

The great love
of an old friend,
the old love
of a great friend
understood, and then
beckoned.

O: that's my SELF
floating before me,
gregarious and grateful,
pressing against my nose
that I never forget to
remember . . .

since the transient,
exhilarating suburban
mirage
will fade me back
unto my fugitive, Humboldt Park

garage.

GLEAM

I and I buckle at the weight of the load.
I and I suckle at the nape of liberty.

I and I rankle at the prospect of servitude.
I and I cackle at the vehemence of zealotry.
I and I seethe from a locus of pain.
I and I breathe in and breathe out again.
I and I ponder every cloud above the swarm.
I and I wonder if the horse is out the barn.

I and I kowtow to the favor of the Muse.
I and I wonder if the feint is any use.
I and I accommodate the pratfalls of desire.
I and I reconcile to wallow in the mire.

I and I dream of a quiet afternoon.
I and I gleam of a truce with doom.

BAD

"I do not want to be friends
or anything else.

I want a complete break
for good.

This whole thing has been bad
from the start."

I'm wide
awake.

I'm not
sleeping.

FUNERAL FOR A BASTARD YEAR

Four stockbrokers took residences in Italy. Four hundred nobodies lost everything. –Charles Dickens, *Nicholas Nickleby*

I know where the bodies are buried:
Lincoln Park before the zoo was there.
Pre-Fire the land with graves was filled.
I move to add our Annus Horribilis.

Sorry, honey, if I don't change the pace.
I can't face another day.
Aspiration upon a table etherized
now embalmed upon a rickety catafalque.

A glass hearse drawn by black horses:
clocking hooves, shrieking springs, yawping axles.
Cheap tin eagles washed in thin gold enamel
preen in effigy on the coffin handles.

Rape, ruin, repossession and remorse.
Grief, gloom, devastation and divorce.
Let the black hooves clock in rhythm.
Let the glass hearse sway in tandem.

Load your rage atop the cheap tin eagles.
Let the rat-bastard corpse rot regal.
Renew, rebound, rejoice and release!
Let the mud-soaked maggots feast.

LIFE

Life is a series of deaths:
self outlasts self outlasts self.
Yesterday remanded to the shelf,
today is the tongue of the bell.

Life is a series of deaths:
resented parents, neglected siblings,
forsaken friends finally become
what they always were: true saints.

To survive is to mourn
in series, in spasms of foul
grief and fleeting eloquence,
a mustering of animal elegance.

Clouds: down of a dove.
Dawn seeds the doves with dreams.
Day is brief, night is grief.
We awaken each morning re-born.

Life is a series of deaths:
of self, of sun, of soul.
And life is a series of songs,
a chorus of hallowed tongues.

But life is a series of deaths
within, too. That is, a stream of selves-
within-selves, neither compounding
nor compiling. Perpetually re-becoming.

Life is a billion breaths
westward leading, still proceeding.
Our selves, like waterfalls,
new every second.

Dawn is legend, dusk is myth.
Mind: a circular universe of divinity.
Cathay dusk is dawn in Carolina,
Bucktown dawn is dusk in Asia Minor.

So life is a series of deaths
and a series of re-births,
each breath a lurching toward refinement,
each death a seeding of divinity,

each birth fresh dew on a dove.

ELEGY FOR STUDS

Listen: voices embroider
the unwelcome November rain.
Wind: mind radio. Radio:
great friend of the solitary.

Listen: my favorite
spoken-word artist
has checked out.

"Peace, peace! he is not dead, he doth not sleep —
He hath awakened from the dream of life — "

Actor, author, blues rider, freedom fighter.
Activist, archivist. Medium, not message.
Lyre of tongues, culling euphony
from cacophony.

The Gil Evans
of the American
folk chorus.

"Begin again and again the never-attainable praising;
remember: the hero lives on; even his downfall was
merely a pretext for achieving his final birth."

"Working" was the paperback
I wore out, re-binding the spine
with greying Scotch tape.

"The Good War" was Homeric,
articulating the soul of a nation
forged in war.

"Voices. Voices. Listen, my heart, as only
saints have listened, until the gigantic call lifted them
off the ground; yet they kept on, impossibly,
kneeling and didn't notice at all:
so complete was their listening . . . listen

to the voice of the wind
and the ceaseless message that forms itself out of silence."

He read your book, he listened
to your music. He drew you out.
Call it: Old School.

Red shirt, red socks? Red
flag! "Call me Red? I got
your Red right HERE, fella!"

Great line about
his FBI file:
"Some funny stuff . . ."

Listen: Mahalia Jackson,
Big Bill Broonzy, a bright
up-and-comer named
Barack Obama . . .

"His is made one with Nature: there is heard
His voice in all her music, from the moan
Of thunder, to the song of night's sweet bird;
He is a presence to be felt and known
In darkness and in light, from herb and stone,
Spreading itself where'er that Power may move
Which has withdrawn his being to its own;
Which wields the world with never-wearied love,
Sustains in from beneath, and kindles it above."

Wind: ancient wire,
maelstrom of desire.
Studs: the Illinois Zephyr.

"The unwelcome November rain
has perversely stolen the day's
last hour

and pawned it with that ancience fence,
the night."

This came to you
from Chicago.

I WANT TO LICK TEQUILA OFF YOUR THIGHS

Mourning Dove,
Town Crier,

Awaken to your
Power.

Sometimes all you do
Is moan

Bloody
Murder!

BUT YOU
PURGE US!

Attend: Your grief
Is your grace!

I'll say it
To your face!

I dream it
Every night, nightmare

Of bliss,
A soft, quiet

Kiss…
Bleed

My six o'clock
Blues.

Liberator!
SING IT AWAY!

Say: Once we all
Bleed

We can
Again

Breathe.

GET THE LIONS

Get the lions
And tigers

From Lincoln
Park Zoo,

Put them
In New Soldier Field

(like putting aluminum siding
On the Roman Coliseum)

And feed them
Aldermen.

LIFE WITH BON SCOTT

"Powerage." I didn't know it at the time,
But it was

"Powerage."

I was in high school, attending Naperville's "Last Fling"
Labor Day carnival. Steel dinosaurs trampled the muddy grass
In Knoch Park. I was waiting in line at the Tilt-a-Whirl.
The ride was run by a grizzled, burly man with tattoos,
Years before they were chic, and then common.
With a pony-tail, years before
They were chic, and then common.

The music assaulted us from large, ground-level speakers
At this most daunting of rides for the average suburban
Teenager. I was transfixed, mute, flummoxed. My ass
Was being kicked beyond recognition. "Man, this sounds like
The Stones!" Two guitars slicing their way through the pocket,
Four hands playing one guitar. The voice, reptilian, like
A crocodile gnashing its fangs, shrieking its way through
A bad acid trip.

Now I know: it was
"Powerage," on 8-Track.

"Gimme a bullet to bite on, something to chew.
Gimme a bullet to bite on,
And I'll make believe,
I'll make believe

It's you."

Got up the nerve to ask the carny who, what, It was.
"AC/DC . . . " So when they came to Rockford Fairgrounds
The following summer ('79), for a July 4th festival, and Cesare
Got us work at the soft drink stands there, we made the
Pilgrimage. "Concessions" meant BACKSTAGE. We did have
To work for it. As we slung Cokes and Fantas to the pressing
Lemmings, once again I felt the low-end violence to my soul.
AC/DC was onstage. "I'm out of here!" I vowed, and stepped outside
To see Angus atop the left speaker column, a shirtless peanut
Monkey shot up on speed, shredding his strings and flailing his
Hair, hundreds of feet above the ground.

Unprecedented. At eighteen, I was a concert veteran. But this was
Unprecedented. Lean, ripped, coiled, burnished burgeoning ballistic
Grooves. Fuck the Babys and, frankly, fuck Cheap Trick. This was
Blistered blues from Holy Hell, lockjawed onto my shrivelled,
Squirelly nuts. Concession=BACKSTAGE. Dear Jesus! Here comes
Angus! "My man! A photo?" No sweat. He was even shorter than me
And that's short. The single most pleasant and sweet-faced rock star
I've ever met. "Concession?" he said in his Scottish (not Australian)
Brogue, seeing my t-shirt. "Yeah, we're selling Cokes . . .
Man, you sure sweat a lot!" He let Cesare take a picture of me with
Him. Cheap Trick was too cool for photos. Chumps.

Later that year, they were at the Aragon. Tuma and I
Drove up from Illinois State, straight to Broadway and Lawrence.
You could see Bon's crank through his jeans from the balcony.
When Angus fell down to spin his way through a solo,
He left a thick sheen of hot sweat on the stage. When he took to his
Roadie's shoulders to solo his way through the crowd, they came up
To the balcony, and as they passed behind me, I gently patted Angus'
Sweaty, zitty back. Center stage: Bon. Acid Crocodile, Preening
Ringmaster, Fang-Tooth Shaman. Bigger records and bigger halls
Loomed as he achieved his Inevitable Hell, and I was there, too,
But if you were tuned in then, you got a chance to get a genuine fang

Scar burnt permanently onto your roiling, ever-teenage brain,
But good.

SILENT SUPERNOVA SYMPHONY

Autumn? Advantage: Chicago.
A tree transmogrifies into
A a silent supernova,

An explosion of
Amber,
Auburn and
Amethyst.

Adjacent to the
Aquarium
At first, then sweeping inland, betwixt

A changeling sky and
A yearning mind.

Ardent,
Altruistic prayer,

Alleviating antipathy,
Accentuating amour,
Auguring atonement.

A corpus of incendiary
Affluence,

A copse of earth-bound
Auroras.

A treasure,
A tribute,
A triumph,

Aspiring to living, breathing
Art.

FIVE BOYS ON A GOLF COURSE

for CDR Dan F. Shanower, USN
February 2, 1960-September 11, 2001

Me Speed and Dan
were in the middle
of the first nine

At Springbrook Golf Course,
Naperville, Illinois, 1977.
We

Sucked. We just wanted
to be together.
Speedy and Dan were

the first new friends
I made in high school, dorks
in the Awkward Age, coming

together from differing
junior highs,
House of Saints and Sinners.

Speedy: Sts. Peter & Paul.
Me: Lincoln.
Dan: Washington.

Over the rough, on the
next fairway, Rod
and Ken (Jefferson).

They were on the
goddam golf team,
Very Big Deal.

I remembered Rod
from when were on the Blackhawks,
the NHL team (Naperville

Hockey League). I knew
he didn't remember me, no
clue who. So, in character,

I start to
hassle him: "Good one, ROD!
Cool guy, ROD!"

Later, he told me his
first response was:
"Who IS that asshole?!"

It became
a familiar refrain!

Over time, we all
came together. When "Some Girls"
came out, we were among

the first in line
at Soldier Field, July 8,
1978.

We'd commandeered Speedy's
dad's lime-green Cordoba,
headed downtown at 2 a.m.

We often used Speedy's mom's
Dodge van, after school,
to Bizarre Bazaar in Old Town,

looking for Civil Defense jackets
and bootleg records (at the time,
I didn't know what a "bong" was).

Graduation: Speedy was
Valedectorian, Ken was
Best Personality, I was

Class Clown (Rod: "I thought
Dan was
funnier").

Rod became Most Successful.
Fast Forward: Rod is at Southern,
Ken has started a business, Speedy

is at U. of I., Dan
at Carroll College, Waukesha,
Wisconsin. My sister called

with the news:
"Speedy died." Aneurism
during a touch football game

on the U. of I. quad.
Five boys became four pall-
bearers and a first friend.

Fast Forward: I'm watching
"Good Morning, America," Sep. 11,
2001. They interrupted

themselves. A plane had hit
the World Trade Center, then we
all watched the second one

hit. I start channel surfing.
Jim Miklawszewski, at the Pentagon,
where Dan was now a Commander

in Naval Intelligence, says
something just hit
the building.

The next day, Rod
called with the news:
"Dan's dead."

"O strong dead-march you please me!
O moon immense with your silvery lace you sooth me!
O my soldiers twain! O my veterans passing to burial!
What I have I also give you."

We who remained drove
a van to Arlington, VA,
for the military funeral,

smoking joints and telling
stories. The Navy
bore pall

for us
all.

ALL SAINTS TRIPTYCH
(HOMAGE TO SKREBNESKI)

No. 1, left: St. Francis of My Ass

I don't mean to tick anybody off.
I pray to my own St. Francis.
St. Francis of My Ass, Clyde!

Nobody but me slams
my door. This keeps me free.
I am not a Socialist!

I am not a bedbug!
I do not weep blood and then cease.
Like an eagle, I increase!

Yes, and this is
an eagle which stands
for itself.

This can be a weird thing
when it's real. This is the deal:
you are the deal.

And sometimes it fucks up,
becoming a veritable bay
of pigs, twigs

in a bastard eagle's maw.
Wait: I didn't mean that!
I meant bats

in a bog-hole.
Ego mistaken for conscience,
ice in a bog-hole.

Who cares if God is dead?!
What make the maw of the moon?
Youch! Intimations of gloom . . .

Don't tell me who God is,
don't bother. Let it hover.
Rat Bastard Moon!

Skull of the frozen lake,
a whirlpool of drama,
skull god strafes lake.

My garden is frozen,
twigs crack by the dozen.

No. 2, center: Son of St. Francis of My Ass

I'm just trying to have a good time.
Hurt is Hell. Let's have a bell!
TONG! TONG!

And a crow.
My Hell is a deep Christian
well in a raw field

just beyond
the edge of the last
suburb.

A raggedy-ass crow,
nothing noble, no Narcissus
of wire. A red crow

in a Hell of black crows.
This kind of thing. The bell
rings

big: Tong.
The heirs of this Christian shell
scuttle all raggedy-ass

through a cornfield of bones.
The bones shake with shells
a raggedy-ass samba

of scuttles to which
the black crows boogie as
the red crow stays stock still.

And this is the Fugue
of my only St. Francis, my lonely
St. Francis, my homely,

groanly, ownly
Bra Francis: Patron Saint of My Ass.
Hero of my heart!

Goin' for broke
(and when you go for broke
you often arrive)!

Keeper of the faith!
I am the deal, I am
the field

and the infinite symphony
arising from it. Crows, bones and bells
are but atoms of me

in moats of time.

No. 3, right: St. Catherine of My Cock

I will never understand.
This is the beginning, and
the end.

I will never understand
what it means to be
a woman.

Attending to customers
with the basest allure, eyes
flashing

like airplane lights,
Cate shattered
my dimension.

It was
devastating
stuff!

She was first god
of the world, first light.
She is raw power.

She filled my cup, babe,
that's for sure. If God is dead,
something is alive!

How everywhere she is!
Warmth, softness, tears, milk and iron.
She said I began sticking my chest out.

This will
always
be so.

The skyscrapers
in the Loop
are the tallest, the richest.

The hoi-polloi
surround them
north, south and west,

all huddling toward
the proscenium
of the shore.

Tonight
the sky-gods are playing!
Tonight's fare stars the moon

as Aries the Rapier,
Moon Cad on the Make,
Hostage to Destiny!

The stars are Chorus
and the clouds Warrior
Arjuna. The lake

the stage,
the river,
the main aisle.

I wrought a drama
for to Galahad
my Catherine,

a bribe for mercy,
a trifle for her majesty's
amusement about a goddess

who vaguely resembles . . .
Catherine?
She sees. She is pleased.

I set the stage. She seethes.
She whispered "I'm nervous!"
and she was In, baby!

Catherine the Great,
Mistress of Pagan Lust,
Queen Slut of Babylon

redolent of
drama, music
and miracles.

"You got
my heart, you got
my soul.

You got
the silver, you got
the gold."

All I had left
were diamonds
in a deep, dark mine.

"We are gathered, here,
today, to celebrate the American Way!
Let the miracles begin!"

Penthouse on a Bog-Hole!
Sky Box on a Gang War!
And then she said: "I want more."

Lo! Behold: Hallowed St. Catherine,
Dew-Faced Convert, Radiant of God
and refulgent with fecundity!

WTF?

GOD?

OMG!

Promulgate miracles, sure, sure:
the poet, the physician, the farmer,
the scientist,

aldermen,
liquor distributors,
online entrepreneurs . . .

Who knows?! Maybe, some day,
a Space Genghis for to ruminate
upon the Martian Ganges!

Before the vows,
my cards were, as they say,
upon the table.

She held back
her Ace in the
Bog-Hole

until afterwards.
"You held back.
You . . . lied."

"I love you," she said,
"but I have to
go . . . "

And then my mind
said something my mouth
did not:

"Then go: go
fuck yourself and go
fuck your 'love.'

Let 'love'
transfigure me into
your stigmatized Saint?!

Jesus!
Are you a woman
or a ruthless, mercenary

little girl?
Grow, as they say, UP.
Or don't, and

just keep
telling yourself
'He didn't love me enough.'

Enough! Aye,
as they say,
there's the rub.

Quantity
is it.
Telling.

Go. Keep
going. Surely, some cad
will cave.

Go. Keep
going and keep
telling."

Don't tell me what I need.
And don't tell me who I am.
I am the night, and the dawn.

I am dew-light on a fawn.
I grew up when I was still
mowing lawns.

She is cool
to me now
and I stay cool.

I will never understand!
I could ruminate with the zealotry
of a convert

and still end up shit-broke
on a creek bank — just waitin' there
for a little more — but

this is not the end.
This is the beginning.
We are gathered, here, today,

sluts, saints and moon cads,
trying to understand.
And it is a miracle.

This will always be so.

WISH YOU WERE BEER

So: you think you can tell
Heaven from Hell?
Swell!
Do tell.

Your husband
Wants me to help him
Go out and
Get

Laid.
"What a wonderful world!"
Men cave, and then
Cheat.
Men cave men

Cave.
"Men are easy," as my x
Used to say.
I wouldn't pay,
Won't pay.
Yay!

Two lost souls swimmin' in
A fish bowl, year ahfta year.
Have you found
The same old fear?

Anymore, I don't care to
Hear. "You caved."
Rave on.
Without me.

Freedom isn't free
But it sure is a
Bargain.
The best

I ever had.
Love is free.

GREAT EXPECTATIONS

It is the best of cities
And the worst of cities.
I checked it out, and I found myself a city

To live in.
WHERE will let me
Be me?

I made a bet. You bet!
I knew I'd need
Big shoulders to cry upon,
Big enough for both

My dirty angels. I knew I'd need space
To spread my brittle wings. I knew I'd need a place
To sing.

When I was just a boy
In Naperville, Illinois,
I thought Chicago was a blown-glass downtown
Surrounded by
A vast, dissipated

Ghetto. Burlington-Northern got me where I need to
Get to: Wrigley Field, Chicago Stadium, the
International Amphitheater. I saw what I could see:

Led Zeppelin, the Stones,
The Foghat, Queen.

Wax Trax, Bizarre Bazaar, eventually

Max
Tavern. I became
What I could be.

Hey: I didn't go
To college. I went to
Illinois State. There, I
Learned that middle-class, heck, even UPPER
middle-class people lived in

The city. Dick Roeper, Mick Caplan,
Randolph

Salerno. Evan, Vinnie . . .
Phyllis', Rainbo, Czar

Bar,
Ola's.
Metro, Club 950, Exit.

Checkerboard Motherfucking
Lounge (hi Mr. Guy! OK

If we stay?).

Souled American . . .
Tribe . . .

Then, I made myself take
A leap

Of faith, a virtual swan-dive
Off the Sears
Tower: I got up

Onstage

In a
Bar,

And read my terrified poem
To a handful of people who came
To watch the hockey game.

Not only did I survive,
I got a FREE BEER, and got out
Alive.

I found myself
I found myself
I found myself

A city
To live in.

THE GREAT BLACK DIAMOND

At the center
Of the universe, at the center
Of the skyline,
Feminine handiwork.
At the center
Of two long, thick, metallic American thighs,

The Diamond.
At the center
Of miles of thrusting
Phalli, the center
Of the visible universe,
Amidst preening, reaching, grasping, often FAILING

Phalli, including the country's
Tallest . . . the ONE building
Everybody asks about,
The ONE building designed
By a woman,
The White Diamond.

Go to the planetarium
And see for yourself.
This time,
Don't take your kids.
Would it be more obvious
If it were pink?

I think
Not.
"What is that diamond-
Shaped building
At the center?"
Yap about the Sears Tower,

Yap about the Trump Tower.
Yap about the Aon Center,
YAMMER about the phalli.
"What is that diamond-shaped building?"
Oh, you mean
The one at the

Center? The ONE
Designed by a
Woman? Careful, there are kids
On the tour bus . . .
"Oh, the Smurfit-Stone Container
Building, from 1983 . . .

When it was first built,
Ice formed on the diamond,
Broke off in chunks,
And landed on the sidewalk
If your HEAD
Wasn't in the way.

So they installed heating pipes
To melt the ice
So it would just
Drip, drip, drip on you, wet wet wet."
Look. See. Georgia O'Keefe
Would be

Jealous. Obvious
Enough?
She trumps Trump.
SHE is the center
Of the visible universe,
The feminine aspect.

Like Trump Tower SLICED OFF
At the base.
Obvious
Enough?
Look.
See.

The center
Of the visible
Universe.
Without
End:
Amen.

LED ZEPPELIN AT THE STADIUM, EASTER SUNDAY, 1977

Minick got grounded
For

Drinking. He sold me
His ticket

For twenty-dollars
In cash,

Walked up to me
In the hallway

At Our Lord
Of the Flies

All Boys Career
Academy

In
Naperville.

SOLD
AMERICAN!

We took
The Burlington-

Northern,
Then the Madison

Bus. "Everybody
Do

The
Madison!"

Same bus
On which

I was slipped
A packet

Of Angel
Dust (which

I ditched
Under the seat),

For giving this
Dude directions

For the Queen
Show. Anyhoo:

Our seats
Were below

The organ.
We had

Binoculars!
The air smelled

Of
Cherry.

Three-plus hours of brutal,
Unrepentant

Rock and
Roll.

Jimmy came out
In black Stormtrooper gear,

Breeches and
Jackboots, pilot's

Cap. Then:
The White

Zoso
Suit.

Half-hour acoustic
Set

In the
Middle,

Smoke-bombs,
Green laster

Pyramids.
The air

Smelled the air
Smelled

Of
Cherry.

PROSPECTUS: MY JIMMY JOHN'S ON BAGHDAD'S MAGNIFICENT MILE

for Kevin Hogan

I'm fired
Up!

I can't wait For Iraq
To be safe For Democracy!
Fellas: make no
Small plans!

I'm openin' me
Up a Jimmy John's
On Baghdad's first
Magnificent Mile!

It's my Brooklyn
Bridge, my Aswan
Damn, my Bratsk
Station!

Help me bring
Freedom to the
People! Let's
Get in there

And start setting up
Those Dan Burnham
Six corner strip-mall deals
And get the neighborhoods

All mapped out
Before Communist China
Figures it
Out and wants

In! You guys: these people
Are going
To have to
Eat! And, no matter what you've heard,

They LOVE
Ham! I'm partial to the
J.J. Gargantuan,
Myself,

But that's beside
The point.
Imagine a run
On Sorry

Charlie's! Fellas: ENOUGH
With the Sentimental,
Post-Modern, Byronic
Ennui!

LET US BUILD! LET US
BRING FREEDOM
TO THESE POOR, BEREFT
MISGUIDED

HEATHENS! We'll put one
Right by where the old
Saddam statue
Was! Perfect

Symbolism!
Send me money NOW!
There's no better
Time to

Save!

I ONCE PRAYED TO GOD

I once
Prayed to God

To
Die.

I once
Prayed to God

For
Pussy,

For money,
For a bus.

I now
Pray to God

For
Mercy.

Only.
Once.

49 WESTERN OWL FEVER DREAM

My secret lover, we
held one another! I kissed
your cheek and then you fell away into a room and then I became another
room and a few people were talking and I felt naked and began to run
back to you room by room
BUT YOU WERE GONE

TO ME

AGAIN . . . then then then I was running through a desert wind farm
going slower and slower and slower
each mill of electricity a lurid pastel and there was a baby sitting
I I I I I became another room and I heard trains
then I fell into a ditch and couldn't get up my knees ached I couldn't
run anymore
whooshed awake God bleary back on the goddam
Blue
Line downtown . . . tumbling . . . ah your
cheek

THE MOON WANES OVER THE LAGOON

A large face of white glare followed me,
Like eyes in a proper painting,

Up Kedzie Avenue
along the west side

Of the park boom boom black summer night, cool blue breeze,
Grand Avenue
a corridor of light like the "Time

Tunnel." I smiled, morphed a bit into James Darren.
Boom that blistered, bald Madonna

Was my spotlight.
I jogged in rhythm with the stoplights.

Boom the black oaks along the lagoon
Became a sighing Stonehenge. The moon waned

Over the lagoon (stop) . . .
and then the earth swayed

Back toward autumn. The black oaks will break out in quiet fire,
then the fire
Will die

and dissolve
into the lawns

I WAS WATCHING JIM MIKLASZEWSKI

I was watching Jim Miklaszewski when the plane
hit the Pentagon. I did not yet know that my friend

Dan was killed. Rod would call
with that "news" the following day. Our hilarious, radical, knucklehead
high-school buddy had become Commander of Naval Intelligence

for the Middle East. Later on 9/11, on the
radio, I heard that the plane hit the Navy part of the building.
I went, to myself, "I didn't hear

that." When the Cole was bombed a year or two before, I was glad that
Dan was safe in the

Pentagon.
On, 9/12, I sent him an e-mail: "You OK?"
We hadn't been getting along so well

of late, and that made me more
worried.

Then, Rod
called . . .

I'm losing it right now . . . shit! . . .

(SHIT!) He was our
friend, and

we miss
him

a
lot . . .

THE ROD BECK BUMMER

Appropo of
nada

I fell
forward

into the
abyss:

Former Cubs
Ace

Rod Beck
indeed

died, Jack
Falstaff

for a double-
header!

Catfish, meat-
face,

passion in
excelsis.

RAINBOW OVER THE ADLER FROM AN OMNIBUS

True story: atop
An omnibus
At the Museum
Campus, after a brief
Shower,
Grinding my teeth

With grief
All day, around and around
In the
Rain,
Grinding pain…
First, Burnham Harbor: a glimpse,

A
Glimmer. Sheen. Then,
Clenching my
Grief
I saw, complete,
A rainbow

Over the dome
Of the
Adler Planetarium.
We all
Saw it,
Momentarily

Transcending
Unbelief:
Exuberant
Relief
Complete: a sea, shards
Of rain, a little

Light.
Boom: in full
Arc, God's
Shimmering,
Shattering
Grace.

THE HAWK

for Guy Adkins

Faces in the bitter cold
crowd:
A frozen bough breaks
under a murder
of sleek crows. Rooks

shriek beneath
the black-winged
clouds.

Red buses whir and whiz,
careening through the sprawl,
black tires bare
with bribes ... say: briared

with bribes. Sign
of the times!
Drunken buses
reeling, poor folk keening

feckless
underneath.
Hawks yet lurk
On the Rookery roof.

This cliff, this ledge,
intercedes between us,
the rust-red dust,
and the Martian
dusk.

The cold hawk scans,
clutching curved
glass, awaiting a collapse,
just one, small fall.

Mine, on the February LaSalle Street
Ice.
The hawk sees,
And waits

to break.

ALLEN GINSBERG FESTIVAL OF LIFE

Just east of Balbo
and Michigan,

Uncle Allen began
his Buddhist

chant. The Festival
of Life

took over
Grant

Park one
weekend the

summer of
'68. Buddha

is at every protest
rally, of

course. Buddha
knows batons

and bullets.
Buddah

feels, he kneels,
he braces . . .

MY GOOD WAR

My friend's father finally
showed me

his medals. His son,
my friend Dan,

a Navy Commader
killed

on September 11th,
had arranged them

in a
frame

some years
ago.

I remember Dan
telling me a story

of his dad laying wounded
in the guts in a barn

in France, but
keep my goddam mouth

SHUT about
it by the way.

In the days
after the attack,

I visited their
home. His dad

answered the door
to their quiet, warm, humble

Naperville home
in tears. Yeah

we wept
some. Then, after conversation and letter reading, suddenly, but quietly,

he brought me
into the dining room.

On the mantel
were his World War II

medals, in a
frame. There were

a lot
of them, I

think more
than Dan

got. "Jesus,"
I thought.

Wide-eyed, dry
eyed, like

I am
right

now.

DEPRESSION

Moon:

BLISTERED MIRROR—

BLACK DOG—

BLEAK KNAVE—

FICTION OF FAILURE—

FUNERAL DAWN—

AIRLESS GUILD—

LOVELESS COVE—

SKULL OF GOD

TO WHOM

ANIMALS

ONCE PRAYED.

MEN MADE OUT OF BIRDS

Behold the Birdman: dove feathers, black eyes, wine-red tail.
Belligerent as the garish sun, Jove-bound to make war.
His cold, dove blood hums. Then, dove-white, lightning strikes.
Blonde smoke billows, black doves dive, then die.
The flock of his body flings mercilessly, hissing.
What pain is his mother? What rain fangs the bleak eyes?
This is the rain that flecks black eyes: the last lust of American Mars.
Thus solitary, and like a widow thus. Cold, light blood. Red stars, plum stars.
Old, cold light. The black blinking sky: cacophony of war widows.
War: rain burns and blood reigns. He taught a tree to see and it learned.
This is the pain that mothers lust. He set a bee free and it burned.

Amplest of Nations, King of Provinces, still in the night he weeps.
Perfidiously his friends have dealt, and are now enemies. Bleak smoke
Shields now the fiends. Bleak might of Jove! Shark bone beak! Black widows

Shriek.

THE CONQUEST OF SHIT CREEK

Black Hawk said "Fuck
This, I want

My land
Back." Beaubien

Thought he'd
Pulled a fast

One, got the Heathens
Drunk, got 'em to sign away

Their land.
Earlier in the day, the Natives

Guffawed that Whitey
Wanted to scalp 'em for

Shit
Creek! Only the French

Could put a whorehouse
On every bank! "Then they'll get us

Get good and
Drunk …"

Dissolve, months later:
Black Hawk is like

"Fuck this, I'm taking
It all

Back." They
Wiped him

Out, but he
Made his

Run.

THE GREAT WHITE DOPE

We collude in a conspiracy of silence.
We intrude on the poor, demanding coke.
The Children's Crusade to re-take Humboldt Park

Commemorated the dead. For every line we do,
A bullet blasts into an innocent child's brain.
But not in Barrington. For every line we do,

A poor family is destroyed. Not in Naperville,
Glenwood or Homewood-Floosmoor, where the children
Do more blow than we want to know.

Their parents have jobs, after all, bills to pay,
Antiques to collect, time-consuming affairs
With neighbors to conduct, this kind of thing.

Hey, raising kids right is really hard!
Sometimes you wanna party. I get it.
Sometimes you wanna party!

I think now of Dylan Klebold's BMW . . .
Perhaps he just needed more Ritalin.
It's hard to raise kids right.

Sweep the schools. The richer the suburb,
The more drugs you'll find there. Shucks,
I must be one ANGRY DUDE! Mercy!

Hey, you guys, just forget I said anything.
I'm just a lonely, bitter, failed malcontent
So you can just write me off and carry on. Besides,

"The Drug War," one of the funniest, most self-affirming
fantasy series on TV comes on shortly so I can just
chill out to that. Hey, you guys, just forget I said

anything! Have a nice party! I know how
tough it can be to maintain a pastoral façade.
Maybe I'll see you after the next local funeral.

We'll party.

THE HEART IS A LONELY FUCKER

Like a Prairie Falcon landing on my breast,
the God inside me clenches, and your face comes
to me.

You have landed, again a waking dream. As in a dream,
setting constantly transmogrifies, details, red-tails fly
at whim.

You are a solid, silent earthquake. As in a dream,
setting constantly breaks apart. I crawl, clutching
grass.

My glass breast cracks. Tonight you shall fly across
the universe, and I will miss you, miss you, miss
you.

The Jack-o-Lantern moon grins falsely askim the glass
lake. This black beach is autumn night which lands
bleakly.

This silent tongue, the lake, laps the cystalline wind,
the dim, gold aura of moon crawls obliquely from the
horizon,

hissing light.

FEED MY STEEL BIRD

I and I, bent on justice,
Have you in

Mind.
Heart flattened by a wind
Lorry.
I and I bide like a hawk on a

Spire.
Sinner, sucker, self-serving
motherfucker: stay out of the park. I and I wait patiently atop the spire of
New
Pru.

My dad played pinochle every lunchtime
At
Old
Pru.

THIS is the voice of GOD:
You're gonna be

Sorry.
Worry: I and I see. I and I saw. I and I
Saw
It all. I'll pierce your soul with my crimson claw. Clever: crime can be silent as

Mind.
I and I are not
Blind.
Lithe: fleet as

Wind.
Silent as shame. I and I listened, I and I heard. Your heart will feed

This
Bird.

BAKER STREET BLUES

Gerry Rafferty's "Baker Street"
was "Our Song."

Me, and Ms. Susan
Lynn Vaugh of Mesquite,

Texas, new to Naperville
Central.

I moved in
fast, moments ahead

of my
reputation.

I'd take her to
the newly emerging subdivisions

in southeast Naperville
after the N-th time

she made me take her
to see "Grease."

My '67 Ford station
wagon had an AM

radio and
a great

back
seat.

Heavy, heavy petting,
fellas.

"Baker Street," "Hot
Blooded," "You're The One

That I
Want . . . "

"Baker Street"
was ours.

Once, while
getting into the back

seat, neither of us heard
the muted thud of her purse

falling softly into
the snow.

Next day, a construction
worker found it,

saw her home address
on her IDs, and gallantly

returned it.
To her

father, who had that day
off. Super.

Thus my adventures
in fiction

began in
earnest.

LIVING IN A LITTLE CATHOLIC CEMETERY

Finally, the whole earth
gushed out of me.
I was left alone, empty, living in a little

Catholic cemetery. Musta been
the southwest side: gangsters, black
atheletes, immigrant labor leaders.

It was
quiet: white dragons, eons of
quietude, short blades of green grass perfectly

kept. One small Madonna, six black
mausoleums. The air was white as
rain.

I was alone but I kept trying
to look like I was
working, always trying

to look like I'm working.
The Madonna was a young girl
with a baby, too young

to be a mother. The girl
was simply much too
young.

The air was bare.
I was warm, but alone.
The dragon was really
an elegant Japanese

lion.

PINDARIC ODE TO THE FANTASTIC FOUR

Ladies: respect. You four came out the front door
at Oakley and North Aves. one late-autumn night
as I lugged the last of my book collection to
Myopic. I was already out of breath, but you guys
took whatever was left. Four of you, ready to PARTY!
One of you said: "We're all wearing short skirts!"
Indeed: short skirts, leggings, knee-high spiky
boots.
Lo: you are better-educated, better-paid and
better-prepared for life than your male counterparts.
Me? I'm a generation

older than y'all. Your power, confidence and obvious
success turns me ON. No threat here. I am a success,
too, but I am poor.
I envy the men of your generation, not you guys. Be
patient
with them. The one you fall in love with might not
make a
great husband. Have joy, then move on. You'll find
what you
need. Hello: I love you. I blew my nose and then
y'all blew my mind. Me? I am off the hook. My
generation has
exceptional women, too, and they have loved me madly.
But your youth, energy, elan and grace hurt my heart.

Then, quickly, it healed,
stronger than ever.
I treasure this. I will never

forget you.

HOW COULD I NOT SEETHE?

How could I not seethe
for the exquisite luxury
of your
skin?

How could I not burn
for the fugitive elegance
of your
face?

My manly quest enslaves me.
Ensnared you, scared you,
beguiled you — like
a bitch cobra —

if only for a fortnight.
That's an English
term. This
is History.

As I wait to die
in failure, fighting
for every inch,
I lie awake praying.

I pray and pray
but God has nothing
to say. No
history.

Just memory:
the scent
from your wrist,
your vicious kiss,

your lemon hair
in the sunlight
at B'Hai
Temple. Two minutes

of mystery, a frontier
of hope, dreams
come to life (to memory
if not history).

Let's remain
anonymous!
Our memory
equals history.

I
remember.
I
burn.

I DREAMED I SAW ST. VALENTINE

I was cornered near Lincoln Park
by the Unholy Three: Gov. Blah-Blah-Blah-vich,
Speaker Mad Again and President Stroker.

They threatened to crank my Juice payment or
take away my buses and hospitals. "Gee whiz,
fellas!" I sputtered as they clenched their fat

fists around my whiny throat. Then suddenly came a chorus
of angels, and a bright light broke through the ashen clouds.
Like a great bald eagle, with the visage of Tony Peraica,

St. Valentine in sandals descended. "Hark, ye Sharks!
The Age of Graft has now ended! Unhand this slave and all who
tremble like him or ye shall wither like a First Ward Republican!"

"Curses!" screamed the Three, in unison and with feeling.
Then I awoke, clutching my throat, still in my orderly scrubs,
late for work again and scrambling for my bus pass.

DUDES

I dream about Scott Tuma*
every night, have for years.
Irrigation, with air.
Dudes: I need

a bike.
Dudes: Less smoke one.

Bunny was a poet named Langston.
He was huge, groovy, for real.
Riffed until the cows came tumbling, crumbling down.
HI BUNNY!
Tread: He intoned the narrative of the wall carving

at the DuSable Museum, late
'80s. Yep: the Gay, Republican 1980s, fellas.
Eisenhower, anyone?

I SHOOK JOHN ANDERSON'S HAND.
He was my MAN!
Then, Tread: he showed us their collection of venally
racist caricature literature
of this Mid-Century Amerigo, an impressive display of
graphic fiction, vile fucking Amerigan cartoons.
L'il Black Sambo in schwaggage. We were mortified.
Tread: THANKS!

Dudes: tighten it up a little.
Take five and count time, the times you were actually
fucking INSPIRED! Yeah, then it passed.
Examine your sins

and step up with a few, fresh
back-up plans. REHEARSE A FINER TOMORROW . . .
Trust me. Like, talk a walk, have a shave.
Aow, Wicker Park milieu?! Marvy!

Dudes!
"Chay-Chay: how 'bout a
Pabst?"

AFTER MIDNIGHT IN THE LATIN QUARTER

At midnight, the weather broke
in two, and warmth gushed in. I and I

were flushed out into the night.
I floated down North Avenue,

walking past a number of selves —
one drunk, hammered, maybe nineteen —

through the Latin Quarter.
Along the blue-black thoroughfare:

dollar stores, Mexican restaurants,
liquor stores, Puerto Rican restaurants,

joyeria, lavanderia, licoreria, supermercado.
Uh, and shuttered gates

where Capitalism
was late.

Another self here holds onto his dreams
tight, that Right is Might, and in

sucking the life
out of life.

Another will shortly attend a synagogue of bright
pain,
then a cathedral

of rain.
"Wish you were

beer . . . "
Hell is given, Heaven seized

from the blue-black
breeze.

Off the thoroughfare, the houses and multi-flats
evoke a soothing, familial, OLD WORLD DIGNITY,

A FUGITIVE GRACE, breeze at your face,
after midnight

in the
Latin Quarter.

GIMME BACK MY BULLETS

Put 'em back where they belong.
I ran to a gangfight and a

classroom broke out. HO-la!
I shouted out

DRUGS FOR
WHITEY!!!

Whitey don't care unless the
dead kid white.

WHOOPS!
Sorry, fellas . . .

This morning on Chicago's Very
Own Champs D'Eleusis, North Avenue,

I walked alongside a funeral
procession. The hearse

silver, head of a
snake, scaled like a pearl-string of

late-model,
mid-size sedans.

Felt
my pockets

for my
bullets. All good!

Schanna boom-boom,
yeah, Sister,

gotta barrel that's a-blue
and

cold . . .

THE GOVERNOR'S WHORE

I think that I shall never see a poem nauseating
as a fake, business-arrangement marriage.

Thank CHRIST the truth comes out once in awhile,
like, nauseatingly self-righteous assholes and their
LOUSY, miserable marriages, with which they seize
the moral

high ground, looking down their noses at single men
and women who just happened to decide NOT TO BE
FUCKING MISERABLE . . .

You can have all the money and power in the world and
still be a fucking bald, homely motherfucker who has
to fucking pay for it. I DO NOT CARE HOW BITTER I
SOUND!

I think that I shall never see a poem hilarious as a
goddam politician finally taking it up the ass in
front of the entire world. No sympathy either for the
wife who rode the wave to power and fortune.

No sympathy. Sympathy rhymes with sympathy, no?
Shit, the rhythm isn't right. NO BIG WHOOP!
MARRIED PEOPLE DESERVE THEIR MISERY!!! Especially
when

they bring children into this world that they neither
want nor raise properly. O, dear, does that rhyme?
Mercy, I better take a time out . . .

MIGHTY SANTO AT THE BAT
(THE CUBS WILL SHINE IN '69)

The Outlook was quite brilliant for the Wrigley nine that day,
my first Official Cuhs game and I didn't have to pay.
The paperboys of Naperville were on their yearly outing,
Ice cream, hot dogs, popcorn, fanatical screaming and shouting.

Destined for the playoffs, the Cubs weren't frightened of Atlanta,
our fearsome starting line-up felt the Pennant all but granted.
The pure green field and outfield vines did shimmer in the sun,
and we paperboys were confident the contest would be won.

A Cub named Kenny Holzmann had been picked to take the mound,
the best infield in baseball had him covered all around.
Santo, Beckert, Kessinger, Ernie Banks there at first base,
Randy Hundley in the catcher's gear as the outfield took their place.

For long the game was scoreless, both teams stuck between the lines,
with one Atlanta long-ball snatched by Williams from the vines.
And then the time had come for Mighty Santo at the bat,
two Cubs on the basepaths, the opportunity was FAT.

Atlanta's sorry pitcher threw what well he would rue later,
to the very wrong Cub he served up a big, fat TATER.
The ballpark then exploded as they watched the soaring goner,
The Cubs had grabbed the lead with Mighty Santo's three-run homer.

The game continued onward 'til it's foregone conclusion,
but the wild pandemonium left me muddled in confusion.
The Cubs and Kenny Holzmann beat the Braves and scored a shut-out,
but the passion in the grandstands had me wallowing in doubt.

I turned to Johnny Wetzel, paperboy extra-ordinaire,
and wondered why grown men threw one another in the air.
Johnny turned to me like I was well out of my wits:
"Come on, J.J. Tindall, the Braves DIDN'T GET ANY HITS!!!"

And so we paperboys got ourselves a lifetime's thrill,
and Holzmann and Ron Santo? Forget I never will!
O: the days before September when our playoff hopes turned bitter,
I celebrate the day I learned the meaning of "no-hitter."

ELEGY FOR WHITE POWER

God favors us
who grieve,

for we have
loved.

Twelve angry men,
losing their cool:

people of means,
of every color,

have moralized cocaine,
just as they did

liquor during
prohibition.

Legalize it: label it,
TAX IT and let those

who need it
register

to get it.
O SHIT!!!

Couple of lines
at the Jimmy Buffet

or Stones concert,
couple of lines in the

washroom at the charity
fundraiser . . .

O SHIT!!!
Couple of lines before

going on
the air . . .

People of means
have already moralized

it. Can we
'fess up?! Course not. Dig:

Twelve angry white
men and their

moral arrogance:
we have MONEY

so we're GOOD.
America is the RICHEST

nation therefore it is
the best.

Sorry, fellas.
Stop the killing, eliminate

the profit motive,
admit to the single largest drug

DEMAND
in the world.

It's a DEMAND problem,
stupid.

Legalize the goddam
motherfucker.

Ooo, don't wanna threaten
White Moral Power.

I SUCK.
As with alcohol, people

of means have MORALIZED
cocaine, as long as their kids

only DO IT in high school
and don't die

from the market
forces that bring it

to them.
Well, coke and Mother's Little

Helper, of course.
O shit, I acknowledged

unsupervised suburban kids
doing their parents presription

drugs because their parents
have other things on their minds,

like, their own
personal gratification!!!

I SUCK.
Grow up. Fess up.

Legalize what y'all've
already

moralized.
Not until YOUR white kids

in the suburbs start
dying?!

God favors us who grieve
for we have

loved White
Power.

In the name of the Father,
Son and Holy

Ghost, I hereby bury
thee.

May only God
have

mercy . . .

A MODEST PROPOSAL

It is a melancholy object to those
who walk through this great city-state
to see the streets, roads and tavern doors
littered with inconvenient and foul-smelling

human debris. As to my own part,
having turned my thoughts upon this
important subject, weary with offering
vain, idle, visionary thoughts,

I fortunately fell upon this proposal:
having to-date perfected the efficient
and discreet distribution of firearms
to our unwanted teens and tweens —

the envy of revolutionary ideologues the world over —
to further provide professional training
in the use of such weapons. Firstly,
to enable these unloved, unsupervised

undesirables to effect with greater speed
their own self-eradication (is this not our wish?!)
and secondly to reduce the collateral damage
to innocent bystanders with no score the settle.

I am not so violently bent upon
my own opinion as to reject any offer,
proposed by fellow tasteful and wise men,
which should be found equally innocent.

Anyone?

MY SILVER SOUL THE SEA

My soul the sea: sucking
my mind from my skull
like a clam
from its shell, draining

my sweet, slow
juice.

Sitting in the rain
at the Planetarium. Falling from the sky:
the saltless sea. On the left, a festival

of architecture, organic sculpture
alight. Mist aglow, the sky giving its ritual
Spring performance, mirrored

in the torguoise sea. Teal, taupe, agate, shale . . .
Gods of Gitchiegoomee blowing
in my ear. Chaos: the dynamo hum
of the neighborhoods a distant sea-shell aria.
Even Olympian ghosts now loom.

Skyline of neon mausoleums. Spiked shoulders,
hog-ghost compendium, glass slicing the northeast
gale.

My lake, my soul, the sea. The west sun dying
in pink and purple, moon-birth shimmering
skull-white. Soul: drift away,

drift, drift away.

Here on the sea
I can breathe, and rain makes Men O' War
of the eastern clouds, sleek and slow upon the
horizon.

The slow sea gleans me,
cleans my bitter

blood,

the glittering
grey gravity

sucking me,

sucking me,

slowly

back to the
hood.

DIVISION STREET: TWO AMERICAS

This side the dark and hollow bound
lies there no unexplored ground?

1986: Ashland to Western,
Freedom Fighter Promenade.
Poets, musicians, crack whores and junkies,
teachers and tradesmen smarting from the

Clampdown, finding communion.
Fighting to be free,
freedom of EXPRESSION, freedom from
OPRESSION.

Zakopane, Phyllis', Gold Star,
Czar Bar, Leo's Lunchroom, Duk's Hamburgers,
Mexican dance bars, the City's Clean Needle

van. Se vende . . . 2006: Boutiques, wine-bars,
banks and condos, Cliche America straining to be
both rich and

hip.

Western Avenue=Division.
Roberto Clemente inaugurates Fresh America.
Paseo Boricua, Freedom Fighter
Promenade, where flags of fire-born steel

wave in perpetuity.

Communion Street, COMMUNITY, "No Se Vende!"
Americans claiming their singular identity, Port
Richard as Plymouth Rock. We remain OURSELVES,
we claim our freedom to SIGNIFY . . .

Two Americas in tandem, one invisible wall,
Freedom's Phoenix Rising past Freedom's glossy

fall.

BARSHOMBA AND THE GREEN BUNNY

"Yeah, man," Mr. DeFourneaux began,
"Me and Barshomba had
the One Love Peace
Band.

You heard of the Chitlin'
Circuit? South Side, you know,
Bonanza, Peppers,
Rock, Castle Rock,

Checkmate, the Green Bunny?
77th and Halsted in the
early '70s. South Side,
you know: Sam Cooke,
Herbie Hancock, Ramsay

Lewis, Minnie Ripperton.
Barshomba had dreads
down to his ass, you know.
You heard of

Hailie Salassie? (FUCK
yeah, man, I'm hip to
Hailie. JAH RASTAFARI!). Anyway, I was wearin'
dashikis, had an afro

(DUDE: I GOTTA see a picture
of you with an afro!)
Anyway, we was goin' to the
Green Bunny to do a gig,

cuz we heard Marvin Gaye
liked to hang out there after
his shows. I was playin'
marimbas, timbales,

congas, bongos, man,
we're loadin' all this shit
in two cars. We get to
the Green Bunny and — man,

I ain't goan lie — the motherfucker
was CLOSED, man, and I mean
FOR GOOD. I was like 'God-
DAY-UM ain't that a bitch!

Well, after awhile, I shaved
off my 'fro, and I don't think
Barshomba liked that, cuz I only
saw him one mo' thyme after

Bob Marley opened for the Stones
at the Stadium, you know,
Barshomba was hangin' backstage
with Bunny Wailer — you know

Bunny Wailer? (Fuck YEAH
I'm hip to Bunny). Well,
anyways, we was also playin'
with Sons of Slum, Bosco, the
Sparkle Plenty Gypsy Band,

they had Chaka Khan playin'
drums with a double-bass, man,
she was BAD, man, you know,
like Twinkie Floorwood from

Funkadelic? Then Chaka hooked
up with Helicopter, then finally
got up with, man, what was the name
of that band? (Rufus, bro.) RIGHT,

man, Rufus, and she had
that big hit, uh, what was
it? 'Tell Me Somethin' Good,'
MAN, they was BAD, you know.

Yeah, we had some good times
until I shaved off that 'fro,
man, yeah, man, ha ha ha . . . "

BRONZE GILEAD

What sticks, sticks.
What sings,

sings.
Faith is the daughter

of a lilac
dusk,

a breach
of blues

with a bit
of bronze.

O yeah: I found
the mind —

and forgot
my life,

this long, strange
cage rife

with strangers.
Faith: every day

I find
a way,

a great song,
a kind word,

a deliriously
beautiful

face.
Grace, safe space,

this kind
of thing.

I find small,
fine lace

here in this semi-imaginary metropolis
littered with strong, silent post-

modern
extravaganzas, delirium

or terror
just a whisper away.

Each day
I find a new

face. I abhor
waste, I adore

silence.
I found the mind

waiting, wishing, wanting,
hissing. Then it paused

for grace:
my daughter

singing quietly
in the

lilacs.

BLACK DOG IN LITTLE HELL

PLEASE God
NOT TODAY: I have to
work! My self-esteem
went to bed in Lincoln Park

and awoke in
Goose Island, Old
Little Hell.
Black Dog

barking: the only Chicago
hurricane, broiling
from within. Blank
pain, rank blood flood.

Night drove a river piling
into my grief reservoir, so
flagrant failures, vicious
insults, and stagnant heartbreak

shatters my smile.
BUT I HAVE TO WORK!
To teach, entertain, lobby
for life! I HAVE TO WORK . . .

I'll have to
lie, to act, to merely
endure (again).
This broken morning

there is no
tomorrow, this broken
moment there is only
snarling sorrow. And I have

to
work . . .

REGULATED MILITIA WELL

after William Carlos Williams

A well regulated Militia,
being necessary

to the security of a free State,
the right of the people

to keep and bear Arms,
shall not be infringed.

A WELL REGULATED MILITIA BEING NECESSARY
WELL REGULATED MILITIA WELL REGULATED

MILITIA
being necessary

the right of the people
to a WELL REGULATED A WELL

REGULATED MILITIA
it tastes

good
to me it tastes

good
to me

A WELL REGULATED
MILITA BEING NECESSARY

shall not be infringed shall not
be

infringed A WELL REGULATED
MILITIA

BEACHWOOD HAMLET

What a rogue and peasant slave am I!
Too-literate malcontent, recorder of deeds:
The laws' delay, the insolence of office.

Yep: sorrows come in battalions, fellas.
Platoons of knave clowns, festooned with
Uncles, o'erwatched by Chinamen. Who now

Bellows "Fie!" upon the squads of Yoricks
Casting false shadows, belching ghastly ballots
From the Dead? Presidents grandfathered by

Murderous incest, mayors crowned by digital
Machines . . . Alas: I am dead. Report me and my
Cause to the unsatisfied. The rest is

Silence.

About the Author:

J.J. Tindall is a Chicago-based, internationally acclaimed poet, musician and recording artist whose first book of poetry, *Joe the Dream*, was published in Chicago by Bagman Press in 1990. His poems have also appeared in journals and on websites around the world, and since 2007 he has been Poet-in-Residence for Chicago's distinguished online journal of politics and culture, the *Beachwood Reporter*. He has given readings across America and Europe, where his recordings of poetry and poems set to music have garnered repeated airplay. He has written, performed and recorded with a number of Chicago-based bands and has two CDs of music, *Men in Love* and *Songs in the Rock Genre*, now available at i-Tunes. He was born in Naperville, Illinois, in 1961, and attended Illinois State University before moving to Chicago, where he has lived since 1986.

Made in the USA
Las Vegas, NV
18 May 2021